D1524230

Wild Animal Kingdom

LIONS

GAIL TERP

WORLD BOOK

This World Book edition of *Lions*
is published by agreement between
Black Rabbit Books and World Book, Inc.
© 2018 Black Rabbit Books,
2140 Howard Dr. West,
North Mankato, MN 56003 U.S.A.
World Book, Inc.,
180 North LaSalle St., Suite 900,
Chicago, IL 60601 U.S.A.

Jennifer Besel, editor; Grant Gould, interior designer; Michael Sellner,
cover designer; Omay Ayres, photo researcher

Library of Congress Control Number: 2016050031

ISBN: 978-0-7166-9363-5

Printed in the United States at CG Book Printers,
North Mankato, Minnesota, 56003. 3/17

Image Credits
Alamy: Aditya "Dicky" Singh,
26–27; Arco Images GmbH / Alamy
Stock Photo, 6; Ariadne Van Zandbergen,
23; Kumar Sriskandan, 12; Getty Images:
Barcoft Media, 4–5, 11; Tier Und Naturfotogra-
fie J und C Sohns, Cover; Shutterstock: Aaron
Amat, 24 (hyena); Alexander Kazantsev, 24 (giraffe); Anan Kaewkhammul, 24 (zebra); David Evi-
son, 21; DoubleBubble, 14–15; Eric Isselee, 6–7, 8–9,
19 (right), 24 (leopard, cub, and lion), 31; FeraBG,
18; GUDKOV ANDREY, 1, 3, 16–17, Back Cover;
Johan Swanepoel, 32; MZPHOTO.CZ, 28; oorka,
15, 19 (left); Petr Masek, 22; Robert Eastman, 24
(chameleon)
Every effort has been made to contact copy-
right holders for material reproduced
in this book. Any omissions will be
rectified in subsequent printings
if notice is given to the
publisher.

Contents

CHAPTER 1

A Day in the Life

It's early morning. Three female lions walk through tall grass. They look for **prey**. Soon, they spot a **herd** of zebras. Slowly, the lions walk closer. The zebras don't see or hear them. When the lions get close, they run at the herd. One lion rams into a zebra and pulls it down. The lion quickly takes a bite.

WEIGHT
250 то 560 POUNDS
(113 to 254 kilograms)

300 350 400
250 450
200 500
150 550
0 — 600
pounds pounds

A Feast

The females start to eat. Their sharp teeth tear into the zebra. Soon, two male lions join them. They push the females aside. The lions eat until only bones are left. Then they leave to find some shade. They'll sleep for hours.

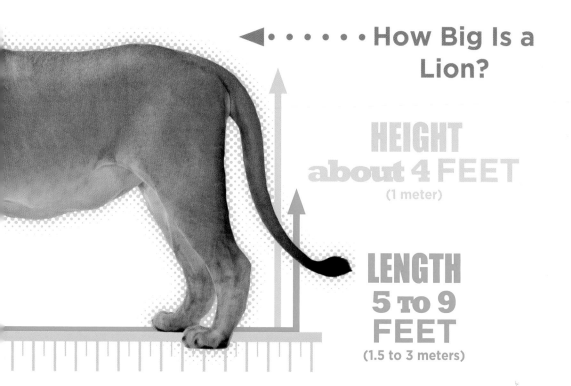

◄ • • • • • • **How Big Is a Lion?**

HEIGHT
about 4 FEET
(1 meter)

LENGTH
5 to 9 FEET
(1.5 to 3 meters)

LION FEATURES

MANE (MALES ONLY)

FUR

TAIL

PAWS

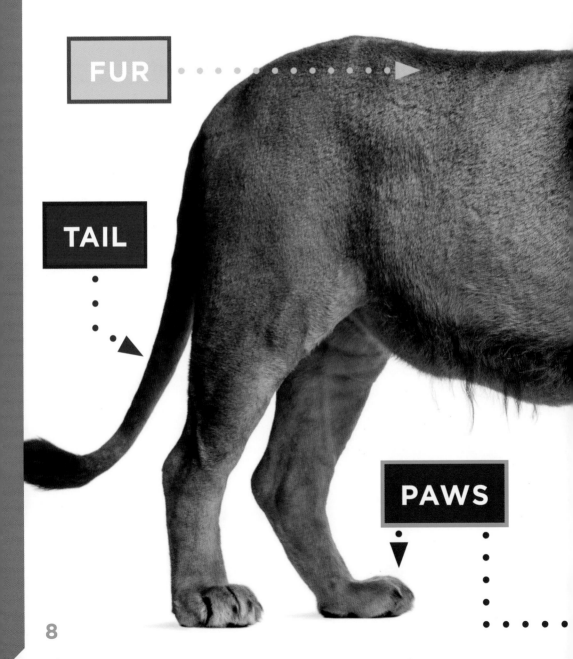

EYES

WHISKERS

SHARP
CLAWS

9

CHAPTER 2

Food to Eat

and a Place to Live

Lions hunt many kinds of animals. They **prefer** large prey. Many lions can feed on one zebra or giraffe. But lions also hunt small prey, such as birds and reptiles.

Females do most of the hunting. They usually hunt when it's mostly dark. Early morning and evening are the best times for hunting.

A LION'S DAY

sleeping	**19 to 21 HOURS**
traveling, hunting, eating, family time	**3 to 5 HOURS**
	hours 0

Home Sweet Home

Most lions live in Africa. A small number of lions live in India too. In 2015, only 523 lions lived in India.

Lions live where they can best find food. They live in forests. They also live in grassy plains. Lions don't live in the driest deserts or in rain forests.

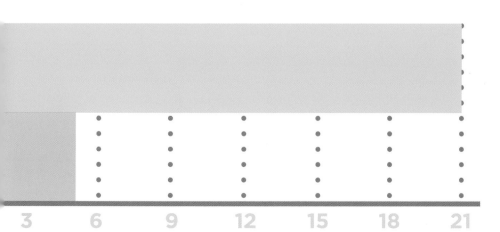

3   6   9   12   15   18   21

CHAPTER 3

Family Life

Lions are very **social**. They live in groups called prides. Prides have up to 40 lions. The group includes females and their cubs. It also includes up to seven adult males.

COMPARING SIZES

Having Cubs

Females have **litters** about every two years. A litter has one to four cubs. Cubs are born in **dens**. Females hide their dens. Hiding keeps the cubs safe until they can walk. In four to six weeks, they all join the pride.

mother
275 POUNDS
(125 kg)

newborn
3 POUNDS
(1 kg)

Growing Up

Cubs follow their mothers everywhere. By age two, they start to hunt.

Most females stay with their prides for life. Males leave their prides when they are two or three years old. Young males often travel together. In time, the group will try to take over another pride.

By the Numbers

10 to 14 YEARS
AVERAGE LIFE SPAN

LENGTH OF LONGEST TEETH
2-8 INCHES
(7 centimeters)

30
TEETH

5 miles
(8 KILOMETERS)
HOW FAR A LION'S
ROAR CAN BE HEARD

35
MILES
(56 km)
PER HOUR

TOP RUNNING
SPEED

Lion Food Chain

This food chain shows what eats lion cubs. It also shows what lions eat.

HYENAS ▸ LION CUBS ◂ LEOPARDS

ADULT LIONS

GIRAFFES   REPTILES   ZEBRAS

CHAPTER 4

Predators

and Other Threats

Adult lions have no **predators**. But animals do hunt lion cubs. Hyenas will kill them. Leopards hunt them too.

Lions sometimes kill each other. Males fight to take over prides. Some lions die during the fights.

Human Threats

People are a threat to lions. Some people hunt them for meat and sport. Others hunt lions to stop them from killing their farm animals.

Humans have taken over land where lions once lived. Lions now have much less land on which to live and hunt.

Lions don't always get prey. A group catches prey about 30 percent of the time.

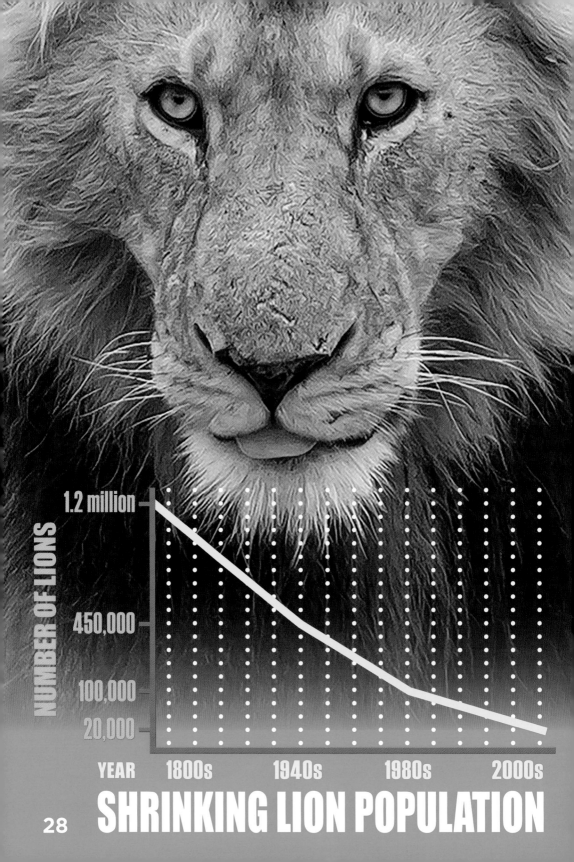

NUMBER OF LIONS

1.2 million

450,000

100,000

20,000

YEAR   1800s   1940s   1980s   2000s

SHRINKING LION POPULATION

Protecting Lions

Lions are in danger of going **extinct**. People are working to protect these animals. People have set aside land for lions. Laws also control hunting. People hope the number of lions will start to grow. Then no one will live in a world without these awesome beasts.

GLOSSARY

den (DEN)—the home of some kinds of wild animals

extinct (ek-STINGKT)—no longer existing

food chain (FOOD CHAYN)—a series of plants and animals in which each uses the next in the series as a food source

herd (HURD)—a group of animals that live together

litter (LITER)—the young born to an animal at a single time

predator (PRED-uh-tuhr)—an animal that eats other animals

prefer (pree-FUHR)—to like better than someone or something else

prey (PRAY)—an animal hunted or killed for food

social (SOH-shul)—liking to be with others

BOOKS

Daly, Ruth. *Lion.* Big Cats. New York: AV2 by Weigl, 2015.

Stewart, Melissa. *Deadly Predators.* National Geographic Kids. Washington, DC: National Geographic, 2013.

Way, Jennifer. *Lions and Other Animals That Stalk Prey.* Awesome Animal Skills. New York: Windmill Books, 2016.

WEBSITES

African Lion
kids.sandiegozoo.org/animals/mammals/african-lion

African Lions In Trouble
www.timeforkids.com/news/african-lions-trouble/188426

Lion
kids.nationalgeographic.com/animals/lion/#lion-male-roar.jpg

INDEX